Michael R. Davidson

The Right to Decide:
Seeking justice for choices around unwanted same-sex attractions.

Michael Davidson, PhD (Rhodes) is co-director of Core Issues Trust, a Christian initiative supporting individuals with unwanted same-sex attractions (SAA) and those who support them. He has worked in higher education for most of his life. He trained for the pastoral ministry, as a secondary school teacher, and until recently was in training as a psychotherapist. Having himself moved away from homosexual practice, he advocates the right of individuals to access professional help to minimise such feelings where possible.

Dermot O'Callaghan, MA (Cantab) is a former management consultant. In his retirement he has taken an interest in the scientific studies that have been carried out in relation to homosexuality. He is a member of General Synod of the Church of Ireland.

Lynda Rose, BA (Exon) MA (Oxon). Called to the Bar, before entering ministry and becoming one of the first women to be deaconed, and then priested in the Anglican Church. She has written several books, for both the religious and general markets, and for a number of years has campaigned on pro-life issues. More recently, she has been involved in setting up Voice for Justice UK, a campaigning group established to protect Christian freedoms and provide support for the vulnerable and abused.

Alan Craig, MBA, BA (Hons) is former chief executive of an international group of manufacturing companies. He is also former warden of an after-care home for young offenders on their release from prison, and former director of a church family centre and former local councillor - all in deprived east London where he lives. He now considers himself a Christian family man, activist, and occasional blogger (www.alansangle.com) who relishes the rich vitality and diversity of his inner-city life.

The Right to Decide:
Seeking justice for choices around unwanted same-sex attractions

Compiled by Michael R. Davidson
Edited by: Dermot O'Callaghan, Lynda Rose, and Alan Craig.
Copyright © 2012, Core Issues Trust

Front cover: Lady Justice overseeing the "Well of Justice" at Frankfurt's Roemer Square, Germany

Published by Core Issues Trust, a company limited by guarantee (NI606015) and accepted by HMRC as a Charity (Tax Number XT29880).
Further information: www.core-issues.org
Copies available: info@core-issues.org

ISBN : 978-0-9573739-0-7

"... we must respect the choices of all who seek to live life in accordance with their own identities; and if there are those who seek to resolve the conflict between sexual orientation and spirituality with conversion therapy, they must not be discouraged.
It is their choice ..."[1]

Douglas Haldeman

1 Haldeman DC. *Gay Rights, Patient Rights: The Implications of Sexual Orientation Conversion Therapy*. Professional Psychology - Research & Practice 2002;33(3):260-4.

Core Issues Trust

CONTENTS

PREFACE

Gay and proud! We're born that way and here to stay…! Game over.

Increasingly, that's the line being pushed in the UK today by gay activists who want officially to redefine sexuality; socially, legally, educationally and politically. But, as the following stories show, that is by no means the whole picture. Whatever is asserted to the contrary, there is a growing body of evidence showing people are not 'born gay', and that nurture and childhood experience play a vital role in determining future sexuality. But, perhaps more importantly, they reveal that some people find such feelings within themselves deeply distressing.

So why should people not be happy with same-sex attraction (SSA)? As the stories demonstrate, there are many reasons. Some people want a traditional marriage and biological children; some baulk at the lifestyle, lived by so many, in particular what can feel the almost exclusive focus on sexuality; some are frightened of the health dangers; and some find homosexual practice morally wrong. In a sense, none of the reasons matters. What is important is that some wish to choose their sexual orientation, and if they need help in achieving their goal, by what right does society seek to intervene and tell them they're wrong?

One must never trivialise these issues, but there are comparable scenarios throughout life where people seek to exercise choice based on 'preference'. For example, a young girl may want breast enhancement, despite the fact the doctors tell her it is completely unnecessary. Yet provided no pressure is exerted, and she is legally capable of giving informed consent, no one would seek to prevent her – indeed, most people would be supportive, because she is exercising her individual choice, and because body image matters and is clearly important to her. Likewise, a physically healthy adolescent may want gender reassignment, because he or she feels 'trapped' in the wrong body. Concerned parents may counsel them to wait, but society today would not seek ultimately to prevent them, if that was what they wanted and chose.

Yet when it comes to unhappiness with feelings of same-sex attraction, instead of affirming the attempted exercise of personal choice, a different set of rules seem to prevail. In the push by gay activists to attain social 'normalisation' and acceptance, this is apparently the one area where it is absolutely *verboten* to express the merest hint of dissatisfaction or unhappiness. In essence, such unfortunates are simply told that they are wrong and, as such, that they have no right to receive help to change.

How is this fair? How does this uphold the rights of individuals to make their own life choices?

Most of the stories in this book demonstrate the major and profound influence of faith on behaviour. Yet what matters here is not the issue of faith, but the individual's right to choose how they want to live. If people decide on the basis of faith to devote their lives to helping the socially deprived, society says that is good, and honours them. Yet if they voice a similar faith based conviction as regards their sexuality and preferred lifestyle, they find themselves condemned. Such commitment to the Bible – or the Koran – is simply a relic of antediluvian homophobia, say the critics, and therefore wrong. Scripture must be either redefined, or ignored.

Yet in a free society any belief, where legal and honestly held, should not be trivialised or suppressed in this way. It is a contravention of human rights.

Some of the ideas and sentiments in the following pages may be controversial, but the fact remains that some people experiencing same-sex attraction feel intense anguish, and want to change. Most important of all - as you will read - with help, they can.

They have the right to choose.

Revd Lynda Rose
Director, Voice for Justice UK

INTRODUCTION

I am often asked by those interested in the issue of unwanted same-sex attraction to introduce them to the men and woman who journey away from homosexual feelings and practice. It is very difficult to arrange such meetings for many reasons. The fact that many of the stories that follow are written under pseudonyms is illustrative of the climate the UK finds itself in today, and indicative of the high levels of intimidation this population group feels in our society.

These people, whose accounts and personal goals are often dismissed, are the subject of repeated stereotyping and pejorative remarks by gay activists. They often speak of how devalued they feel by the professions that have abandoned them, the church which fears them, the politicians who ignore them, and increasingly hostile activists who despise their accounts. They also speak of an enduring fellowship between themselves and those who walk alongside them as fellow travellers, mentors, therapists, counsellors and pastors.

Each of these individuals, bar one, is known to me personally, either through interviews, counselling, psychotherapy and support group sessions, or because they are my friends. All are resident in the UK or in the Republic of Ireland, and their average age is 31 (between 23 and 55 years). Five come from Northern Ireland. Five contributors are married, one recently and another has remained so for 32 years. Among their number are a mother, youth workers, ordained ministers, dentists, a doctor, a project manager, an HE lecturer, a lab technician, and a salesman. The vast majority (all but 3) have been exposed to professional psychotherapy of some sort or other - and some of them to what gay activists and an unsympathetic and sometimes uninformed media refuse to describe as anything other than "reparative" therapy. Only one member of the group has actually undertaken what is properly termed Reparative Therapy©, under a therapist qualified to use that modality - which was effective for him.

This book provides a space for such voices to speak their truth from the safest position they can find: anonymity. The majority unapologetically hold orthodox Christian convictions, but do so intelligently and meta-cognitively. There is mostly, in these accounts, a notable and refreshing lack of labelling of the over-played and outmoded "gay" and "straight" binary view of sexuality. Instead, these voices convey the complexity and vulnerability of human sexuality. The echo of a deep anger against early and severe childhood abuse is evident in some accounts, whilst in others there is no attempt, or need, to understand the origins of the homosexual impulse.

Some contributors to these accounts have never acted on their homosexual desires and, because they value chastity or hold to their marriage covenant, will be accused of being inauthentic or, to use the new pejorative, hiding behind 'asexuality' as an unintended consequence of their choices. Those who speak of trauma and childhood abuse have not been especially chosen for this publication to make a point, and yet we should not be surprised that they wish to make a point through their ordeals. Some of the journeys recorded here are incomplete, with respect to the outcome of the walk towards heterosexuality or away from homosexual attraction. But all of these accounts resoundingly speak with a common voice: that it is they, and they alone, who will decide how they will live their lives. They will decide who will support their goals and, irrespective of whether or not they hold to any faith, the nature of the personal identity they will lay claim to and offer their communities.

There are many groups in our society who remain unrepresented in such a collection of convenience-sample stories. For example, women journeying out of lesbianism, or who find themselves on the other side of a period of same-sex interest, are not represented here. The voices of individuals who, as children, grew up in homes with same-sex parents, or those in circumstances where one or other parent left to begin a new life with a same-sex partner, are not heard. The voices of those women shamelessly accused of bringing about their own difficulties in 'mixed' marriages, by allowing themselves to be attracted to, or deceived by, men who were duplicitous in their sexual proclivities, are also missing from this set.

Similarly, women married to men who are, or were same-sex attracted, and who are stereotyped as downtrodden, mindless and trapped, are also a deserving group, whose voice will need to be drawn out to contribute to a more robust description of the ways insensitive gay activism influences opinion against them.

There is no doubt that accounts are readily available of children who speak positively of same-sex parenting, or whose distress at parental infidelity is equally painful, whether the dalliance is with same- or other- sex partners. There are clearly many women who have been deceived by misguided, or wrongly advised men who marry to medicate their sense of inadequacy. These stories are often told as if, in every case, tragedy is precipitated because society has conspired to deny people their freedom of choice: because of systemic, societal "homophobia". Had 'gay' been identified, encouraged, celebrated, normalised, promoted, and supported, it is claimed, none of this would ever have happened.

I am not so sure that the complexities of human relationships are likely to be simplified by broadening the notion of marriage, as the barriers of traditionalism are "torn down" and values sacred to the majority are reinterpreted for, and by, the few.

It is true that any self-respecting society will respect difference and tolerate diversity. Yet my own conviction is that this new society in the UK, in its determination to redefine marriage, family and parenting, is about to disrespect profoundly and to violate individuals who have chosen, or will choose, for the multiple reasons evident in the following stories, to walk away from homosexuality. This is simply because it refuses to recognise their dignity and right of choice. Sadly, those who were once victims have become the aggressors, as gay rights advocacy groups, increasingly and vociferously present in professional bodies, agitate against the right to choose identity, to modify sexual preference, and to preserve sacred or personal values intelligently held, above the emerging values of pansexuality. Yet as the stories of these brave men and women demonstrate, no government, advocacy group, professional body or political party will silence their right to determine their own futures.

Their voices are to be valued and respected.

Mike Davidson, Co-director,
Core Issues Trust

Kevin: I'm not religious, I just don't like it

"The main reason I have chosen my journey is because I have never been happy ... there are many people out there who are not religious but are desperate to get out, but we don't hear from them."

I am not a religious person. My family are open-minded and wouldn't have a problem if I wanted to live as a gay man. I am in my thirties, with two brothers and a sister. My bigger brother and I never had a good relationship, mainly because he felt that our mother gave all her affection to me rather than him. I was very close to my mum but not my dad - I never had a good relationship with him. He is an alcoholic, so we didn't spend much time together. But now that I live far away from them, we are closer, and when I go back home we all spend quality time together.

School was never a good experience. I had one or two good friends, but not many. I have always been shy. I wasn't good at sport, and was always left to one side, as I wasn't good enough to play in the team.

My problems all started when I was about eleven years old, when I was abused sexually by my uncle for five years. I used to spend my school holidays at my grandmother's house. He and I shared a bed and I remember him touching me all over my body at times. Then I just let him do whatever he wanted, and after a while I started enjoying it. I kept it all a secret, and never told my parents. This went on for several years, until one night, around age sixteen, I decided I had had enough of it. I was feeling so low. That night, as he started touching me, I pushed him away and told him I hated what we were doing and it should stop. He tried to convince me, but I never let it happen again. Then for a while I became involved with a male friend, which I thought was only fun.

It didn't happen 'properly' until I was twenty-four. I started meeting guys when I came to live in London. It was a Saturday night and I was bored. I had a couple of drinks in a straight bar first and then went to Soho. I met a guy who was a lot older than me and went with him to a gay bar and then on to his place. The next day was the worst feeling in my life. Yet though I was feeling bad, this did not stop me from meeting him again, especially when I was drunk. Then I became like a sex addict....

The main reason I have chosen my journey is because I have never been happy. It has been a frustrating life, and I have found that I could not cope at all with my emotions. I used to spend most weekends in gay clubs and bars, hanging around with gay people. I would get drunk and do stupid things which I always regretted afterwards. Sometimes I would feel dirty and even suicidal. Words could never describe how wild and disgusting my life became at that time. I came to realise that it was all about sex, and no feeling was involved. One day I would be with one person, and the next day with someone else. I did not find it a normal way of life and always held back from getting involved in a long term relationship – which I know for a fact that I would never be happy in. I have always wanted to have a family with kids, and realised it would never happen, if I carried on with the lifestyle I was living. I have also been concerned over sexually transmitted diseases.

I was not only involved in same-sex activity; I was also going into drugs. Then my life became a kind of hell. I would sometimes wake up in the morning and would not want to look at myself in the mirror.

I wanted help, but it was difficult to find the right person. I was scared that my friends would judge me or reject me. So many times, they would have a conversation about gay people which made me very uncomfortable. Often when we would go out to dinner, they would have their girlfriends and I would be the only one on my own. These situations made me realise how much I wanted to get out of my same-sex attraction problem. There came a point when I felt that I had to stop meeting my friends and stay away from them completely. I have missed them so much, but I didn't want to have a double life. Yet staying away from them has not helped me.

Eventually I was so desperate that I decided to look for a therapist. I did see one who just told me to get over it. That was no help to me. Once she told me that, I never went back. What I needed was someone to help me to leave my old life behind and start again. I now have a support group. It's good to be with people who have the same difficulties, people who accept you and understand your feelings. This made me realise that I was not the only person suffering in silence. And not all people who want to get out of homosexuality are religious. I have met other people who are the same as me – they are just not happy. Maybe there is more support for religious people, so that it comes across as if they're the only ones who want to get out. The media play a big role in that. But I am sure that there are many people out there who are not religious, but are desperate to get out; but we don't hear from them.

I now have people around me for support and feel like a man amongst men. This has given me hope. I drink less and go out with my supportive friends. When I see my friends getting married, or living with their girlfriend, it makes me realise how much I want to be the same. I've met other people who have done it and are very happy – why not me? I have a mentor who has been through the journey and is now happily married. We speak once a week on Skype, which helps. I would like to find a professional therapist experienced in same-sex attraction. I will surely find one, though maybe I'll have to go outside the UK.

Anthea: The abandoned wife and family

"The gay community congratulates him on what he has done – and helps to ease his conscience – despite the fact that he has destroyed the lives of his own family, who were once so dear to him and to whom he owed a primary duty of love and care, even above his personal desires."

When I married Jim, we loved each other dearly and I truly believed that we would be together for life. We were very happy together and I was over the moon when James junior was born. Then when little Molly arrived, our family was complete.

For a while, all was well; then one day I heard a rumour that Jim was spending a lot of time with a man who was openly gay. At first I didn't believe it, but after many evasions and denials, Jim eventually admitted that he was having an affair with another man.

I was devastated. What could I do? If it had been another woman, I might have been able to compete and win back his love. I still wanted to have him back, but the thought of him having sex with another man was very hard to come to terms with. We still had some intimate times together, but on these occasions I felt a deep sense of uncleanness because of what I knew he had been doing with his man friend. I can only leave it to the reader to imagine how violated I felt.

Eventually Jim decided that his own self-fulfilment was more important to him than his family, and he left us to go to live with the other man.

Since then my life has been very hard. Jim and his partner are well off, and enjoy a good life, while I have to struggle to make ends meet. I'm sure that, other things being equal, I could get by somehow or other. But other things are not equal. My greatest anxiety is that James junior feels a sense of insecurity in his identity. His father left us when he was too young to understand. But he was not too young to feel the pain. And now that he is older, he suffers psychological distress as he tries to relate to young men and women of his own age. He has had to have professional help, and he is not yet out of the woods. He hasn't been able to hold down a secure job and I worry about his future. He does not want to grow up like his father, but wonders if he will do so. And although Jim still sees him regularly, he does not treat him as a father should treat his son. Though Molly seems not to have any particular problems, James is not getting the start in life that he deserves.

And I have a feeling of being cheated not only by my husband but also by society, who seem to be so influenced by gay activists. It is unfair that if a man leaves his wife for another woman, society usually strongly disapproves, whereas if he declares himself gay there is somehow a feeling that it is legitimate for him to follow his desires. The highest priority seems to be not the commitments he made on his wedding day, but rather that it is acceptable for him to seek self-fulfilment no matter what the cost to his family. And the gay community congratulates him on what he has done – and helps to ease his conscience – despite the fact that he has destroyed the lives of his own family, who were once so dear to him and to whom he owed a primary duty of love and care, even above his personal desires.

If a man feels attracted to another woman, the honourable thing for him to do is to seek assistance from a marriage guidance counsellor or therapist to help him to reduce his sexual feelings for that woman and remain faithful to his wife; he will rightly be given every assistance to keep his marriage intact. It seems, however, that if he has an affair with a man rather than a woman, therapists are forbidden to help him to keep his marriage intact by reducing his sexual feelings for that man. That is so wrong, and so hurtful to someone in my position. Why should the 'equality' argument lead to the bizarre situation whereby therapy is encouraged in the one case and denied in the other? Where is the equality in this?

I would like to think that another man in Jim's position would try above all to reduce his same-sex desires for the sake of his wife and children. And if the powers that be do not allow that kind of therapy, it is nothing short of an injustice. Women and children will suffer.

Joe: Not 'born gay,' but sexually 'bent' in childhood

"If I am not happy with my sexuality, I should have the right at least to explore the possibility of change"

I am 49 years old. I grew up in a Christian home, and became a committed Christian when I was thirteen. I rebelled for several years in my late 20's and early 30's, but came back to the Lord after almost killing myself. Those years are a period I am not proud of. I did a lot of stupid things and hurt a lot of people along the way.

Right now, I am a work in progress, still struggling with same-sex attraction. I don't think I am intrinsically 'gay', but I have had a very strong fixation on beautiful male bodies - the "Male Model Type" or the "Rugged, Craggy Type" - since I was young, growing out of issues of my own low body-image and self esteem, and this has led my thought-life down some strange paths. I have always been small and very thin, I have a physical deformity which although not obvious when clothed, is apparent when I take my shirt off. So my body is not very attractive. I admire beautiful male bodies, because I wish I looked like that!

I was sickly as a child, and kind of dominated by my mother. She still tries to dominate me, whenever we meet - I'm still her "little boy". My father was a good man, and a keen Christian, but had to work long hours (he owned his own business) and was deeply involved in church activities, away every night, so I guess I never really connected with him. Also I was bullied a lot by my younger brother, who was a lot bigger and stronger than me. This all combined to make me really doubt my masculinity, hence my fascination with "masculine" men. One of the areas of temptation I struggle with is the Internet, and the many kinds of images that can be found on it. That is why I do not have a computer of my own - I use the library, or occasionally internet cafes. I always want people around, to dissuade me from looking at anything unedifying. I even had all internet access blocked from my mobile phone.

I have only twice engaged in homosexual activity (oral sex), many years ago. I still have fantasies of being intimate with a muscular young man, but I've never since acted on those fantasies, although I have come close to it.

If you want to label me, I guess the most accurate tag would be "bisexual", since I am also strongly attracted to women; but maybe slightly scared of intimacy with them. I have never had any sort of real relationship with a woman, although there have been a few women I have met, where there was some sort of 'chemistry'. Nobody in my family knows about my struggles. I have told a few people in my own church, and maybe half a dozen friends from a couple of other churches.

I want to deal with this issue for several reasons. Firstly, I don't believe God made me this way - I was not "born gay". I was born heterosexual, but my sexuality got a bit bent as a result of my experiences in childhood, and the resulting issues of self image and self worth. If those underlying issues are dealt with, I think much of my longing would go away. I long for a relationship with a woman, whom I can love and who can love me.

Secondly, I believe that a gay (or bisexual) 'lifestyle' would be incompatible with my Christian faith. I believe that God instigated marriage between a man and a woman, and sex in any other context is not right, no matter how good it feels. No amount of arguments from gay rights activists will change my mind.

I also feel that if I am not happy with my sexuality, I should have the right at least to explore the possibility of change. I know I am treading on controversial territory here, but I should have a right to explore possibilities and make my own choices. I have engaged in group therapy in the past, which helped me a great deal, while it lasted. Unfortunately, it folded because the numbers in the group dwindled until the group dynamic didn't work properly. I am involved now with a support group, and I find it helpful and liberating to talk openly with people who also struggle in this area. I am also about to start having some counselling. I have a long way to go yet, but it is wonderful that God loves me, with all my flaws and struggles, and that He is always with me and will never leave me.

Edward: Choosing to hold my family together

"The roots of my homosexuality lie in sexual abuse by men as a child, and rejection by my male peer group at a formative time in my childhood."

My story begins at age four when I was sexually abused by a man who was a neighbour. Being so young, I didn't understand what had happened, but during my childhood I had sexual images from this event which no child should have. When I was six, I was seriously ill and missed a year of schooling. When I returned to school I was physically very weak, very thin, and had to wear glasses. The boys in the boys' playground refused to play with me, so I had to play with the girls in the girls' playground. This lasted about a year during my childhood. I felt my father was emotionally distant. I felt he was a bully, but conversely my mother smothered me.

I had no male role model in my family whom I identified with or respected, and I was mostly rejected by my male peer group. As I entered puberty, I began to realise that I felt no attraction to women but was beginning to feel attracted to men, particularly male sports stars and authors. Then at age fourteen I was sexually abused again, by a male menswear assistant in a changing cubicle, while buying a pair of trousers. I felt traumatised, and I felt terrible guilt that I didn't stop him, but I responded to him sexually at this point. I felt full of confusion about my sexuality.

I went to university and met a young man of my own age who was everything I wanted to be, but wasn't. He was strong, sporty, good looking, full of self-confidence, and obviously adored women. For the first time in my life I fell in love. I was shocked at the intensity of my feelings and it was then I realised I was gay.

At this point I felt 100% gay. I had never had any sexual feelings for women up to this point. I began to feel a revulsion and self-loathing at what I was. I didn't want to be gay at all. All I could see was a lifetime ahead of frustration and broken relationships. I kept all this a secret of course. The man I was in love with knew nothing about my feelings.

Then I met some Christians who told me Jesus can take away my sin. Other gay people will disagree with me, but I knew my homosexuality was an inclination to sin, and, as outlined, had been caused by other people's sin against me as I grew up. I repented and begged God to take it away forever. I felt it was dead with Jesus on the cross, and now I could live a new life with faith in Jesus.

I felt complete inner peace. My love for John turned into a normal man to man friendship. I made many new friends male and female and for the next three years I didn't have a single homosexual thought and I believed that Jesus had healed me. Then eighteen months later for me a miracle occurred - I fell in love with a girl for the first time. This was the first of several relationships with girls until I met my wife to whom I have now been married for over thirty years. At this point I would have said I was 100% heterosexual and Jesus had healed me. However life is never that simple.

I decided not to tell my wife of my former problems before we married, which I now realise was a mistake. We moved to a new city after marriage; my network of supportive Christian friends diminished and I began to feel isolated. My wife developed a depressive illness, then had a miscarriage with severe health problems afterwards. We eventually had two wonderful children. All during my marriage, 'bubbles' of the old way of thinking about attractive men surfaced and I realised my homosexual inclinations were still there. Sad to say, because of feeling isolated and unloved by my wife and family, I began to frequent gay internet sites and chat rooms in my 40s, and began to frequent areas of the city where gay men were to be found.

I then had a brief homosexual affair, which I now know was a terrible mistake and betrayal of my wife and children. The man was a sexual predator and cared nothing for me as a person. I thought that because it was a gay relationship, I wasn't being unfaithful to my wife. This I now know to be a lie. My wife and family found out and this caused extreme stress to both my children, especially the younger one. Years later, my wife and elder child have forgiven me; I don't think my younger one has, and it has damaged our relationship. I now realise I truly love my wife and children, so I reject any future unfaithfulness with a man or a woman.

As you can see from my story, my sexuality has been fluid. Perhaps you could say I'm gay at the moment, but I would say I reject my homosexual proclivities, although they are still there. If my faith in Jesus was as strong as in my early 20s, I know they could disappear.

I think it is important that young gay people hear stories like mine and many others like me. Gayness is not written in stone, and they can choose not to express that part of their inclinations. The 'official' line in society is that if you are homosexual that is 'who you are', so accept it. Various options are given to you, such as joining organisations which advocate being 'proud 'of your homosexuality, and even celebrating it.

Nothing is ever mentioned about the other side of this lifestyle. Certainly amongst men there are major health issues, not only AIDS, but permanent damage to various parts of the body. All kinds of sexual deviancy are very prevalent among gay men. A monogamous lifelong faithful relationship between two gay men is rare.

Having children is only possible with a surrogate and, if a girl is produced, how can two gay men help her as parents when she approaches womanhood? And if a boy – how can he grow up not knowing a mother's love? A child has a right to a mother and a father, and I think it is selfish to deny a child this right.

I know that the roots of my homosexuality lie in sexual abuse by men as I was growing up, and rejection by my male peer group at a formative time in my childhood. How dare society tell me there is no way out of my homosexuality!?

A few years ago I asked to be referred to a psychologist, who basically advocated that whatever I felt, was 'right' for me, and that that was fine. There was no moral compass whatsoever; if I had said I had wanted to have sex with two or three men at the same time, that would have been fine.

Some gay people do have genuine loving gay relationships and they choose to go this way, but they should not condemn people like myself. I have been condemned by gay people: "you are really gay" and by straight people: "you are pretending to be straight". The truth is, I am a happily married family man, who chooses to reject his gay side.

This intolerance by some in the gay community towards people like me is unacceptable. Information should be available, particularly about the many causes of homosexuality, and how to get support. People like myself need to be accepted by gay and straight people alike, for who we are.

Phillip: The molested child

"If the counselling community were to accept that your sexuality is not fixed, but formed by events and background, then they could help people"

I am a husband, father, pastor. I am well into my fifties and I would say that it is only in the last two years that I have made any progress with my struggle with same-sex attraction.

As a baby, I was placed into a care home in which there were boys and girls of all ages. It was there that my sexual abuse started. My earliest memories are of one particular older girl taking me aside to play with sexually. I was so young and could not understand what was going on but had a sense that it was not right. This abuse continued for an extended period and eventually I was moved into an all-boy part of the home. I was among this group of older and younger boys for the next ten years, and sexual abuse started with older boys. Masturbating the older boy was the common feature. I again knew this to be wrong, and was at first very scared in case I would get into trouble. But as time went on I found I wanted to engage in mutual masturbation. This became a feature of early and late teen life. Eventually I left the home and started to work and make my way in life, but I had this deep dark secret – that I was sexually attracted to other guys.

My Christian faith convinced me that this attraction was wrong, but this did not stop my sexual cravings. I eventually married and had children, but the same-sex attraction did not go away. I would turn to pornography to feed my attraction and, when my wife discovered this, life became harder. She was repulsed by it. I felt ever more guilty, and that drove me deeper into myself and gave me a stronger desire to ease the shame and depression that I got from the porn. So it became a vicious cycle of abstaining from porn, slipping back into it, then shame and repentance again.

I had read many books to try to help myself; I tried praying harder, but I did not make any progress out of my intensely lonely struggle. I could not share it with any one and that, I think, was part of the problem. As long as I kept it secret, Satan had power over me. I was scared of someone discovering that I was having these issues. Having a very low opinion of myself to begin with did not help. When the struggle got very bad, I began to reach out, and found a Christian group who helped same-sex strugglers, but I was convinced that this sin was so bad that it was not a "normal sin".

There was another incident with porn, and my wife described me as "sick". In desperation I became determined to get help and so began counselling. The counsellor was not a Christian, but he did help me enormously to become more assertive in my dealings with my wife. Whether this was part of the issue or not I cannot say, but I was intimidated by her and lived with her approval as my big goal. When she was aggressive or moody, I was not strong enough to confront her, but let her verbally and emotionally abuse me. This counsellor helped me to stand up against her, and not allow my same-sex attraction to be a stick to beat me with, but rather to bring my struggle out into the open. Along with that, I began to see homosexuality and same-sex issues as not the "sick sin," but just another temptation to overcome. Bringing same-sex attraction out of the 'gross sin' category, enabled me to see I was not some sick soul, but a Christian with a particular sin struggle.

I was not surprised that the counsellor did not see having same-sex attraction as a problem - best just to accept it as part of who you are and live with it. Having read a little in the area, I knew that his understanding was wrong, even though he was the counsellor. I just took what was helpful from the sessions and moved on. Knowing that the Bible called homosexual practice sinful, I knew that there was help and hope, if I could just get someone who saw this issue from a biblical and grace perspective.

I began to be open with a friend who had come out of a similar struggle, and with his help I began to see hope and acceptance. I was more than my sexual struggles, I was growing toward the light of God's word and I could have hope that even if I were to struggle with this issue for the rest of my life, God loved me and brothers accepted me.

Over all the years I was confused about men! I found myself being insecure around them because of my issue and was scared in case I would be sexually attracted to them. My friend advised me to join men's groups and get used to being around men in a natural context. My formative years around my own gender had not been allowed to become a normal part of growing up, because of the sexualisation of these relationships and my inability to relate to members of my own sex in a non-sexual way. What I now found was that the more I mixed socially and emotionally with men, the more the sexual attraction waned. Just that realisation has liberated my life. I have now joined some local societies and have found more freedom in the ordinary relationships in those groups. I cannot say that the struggle is over, but I have had more hope in these last two years than ever in my whole life. Talking to godly and mature strugglers has been the key to the progress I have made on the road of hope.

If the counselling community were to accept that your sexuality is not fixed, but formed by events and background, then they could help people with this issue. If they are unwilling or even forbidden to do so, then strugglers will not get much help from such a group. There is a need for more Christian counsellors in this area, so that fellow Christians who have such struggles can be helped.

It is a tragedy that professional bodies are increasingly refusing to support therapists who help people who want to reduce same-sex attractions, because of a presupposition that sexuality is fixed. What they are doing is leaving such people in despair. I am glad that I met a Christian counsellor who was willing and able to help me.

Mark: A transformed man

"As I can testify, there is transformation from same-sex attraction and homosexual desire; these are not areas of someone's life that they have to simply live with if they do not wish to."

I began to question my sexuality and recognise a difference between myself and my peers around the age of twelve or thirteen, as puberty hit; however, my feelings of being different somehow reached further back into my childhood. I finally came out of "the closet" around the age of fifteen.

I openly lived as a gay man for over twenty years, in which time I experienced every aspect of being in the gay community, and for twelve of those years was in a relationship with a man. During this time I vehemently argued that my homosexuality was a part of me - that it was not a choice, but was something that I had been born to be.

That was until an October evening in 2008, when I had an experience of meeting with God and began to attend church and experience a personal relationship with Christ. Throughout this time, not one of the congregation or the pastor challenged me on my sexuality, or life choices; they simply loved me and welcomed me into the family of the church. However, God was not as quiet on the subject. Over the space of three months He brought gentle conviction to my heart, and over several weeks of prayer, the Holy Spirit brought me revelation over all of the subconscious and unconscious events and decisions that I had made during my life, that had led me to embrace a homosexual lifestyle. He brought me understanding that I had not been born gay, but had become gay, and that it was never his intention for me to have that lifestyle - and how much more he had for me, if I would allow him freedom to heal and transform my heart.

I can testify that over the past four years God has taken me through many past areas of my life and led me gently through a time of healing. This has been through personal time with him and in prayer, but God has also used many other vehicles to enable inner healing of issues that had led me into a gay lifestyle, and also to manage the outward expressions of sexual desire.

One of these vehicles that God has used has been one-to-one counselling. Whilst this hasn't always been easy or pain free, it has brought me into a greater freedom. I realised my sexuality was not my identity, but I had been identifying with my sexuality. This is no longer true; my true identity is in Christ, and through Him I am a new creation and am happy and fulfilled in His new purposes for my life. I have been released from the things that kept me bound in homosexual desire. Christ has led me through the misunderstanding that I had, and is now equipping me to help others in similar situations who wish to seek God and relinquish their same-sex attractions.

I am appalled that many counsellors or therapists are being told that they cannot assist clients, who may decide that they wish help in dealing with same-sex attraction and homosexual desire. We may live in an inclusive society, where each social minority has equal rights (and rightly so). But this should also be allowed to include those individuals who choose to seek help.

Today, with political correctness, we think of homosexuality in the same category as race and disability, but it is not. Race and disability are things that the individual cannot change, whereas sexuality can be changed. We do not bat an eyelid when we encounter individuals who after being in a heterosexual marriage and having children suddenly decide they wish to change their sexuality, so why are so many people in uproar if an individual who has same-sex attraction wishes to cease being so?

And is it not a responsibility of professionals who work in counselling and therapy to help those who struggle in this area of their lives – those who recognise that they were not born with a homosexual gene (there is no scientific evidence anywhere to support this claim), and who wish to find a way to overcome their desires, finding healing for those areas that may have led them to develop same-sex attraction? To deny them this right, is denying them their individual right to decide their own life choices. As I can testify, there is transformation from same-sex attraction and homosexual desire; these are not areas of someone's life that they have to simply live with if they do not wish to.

Robert: Through childhood abuse and adult despair, to freedom

"My homosexuality was the result of serious dysfunctional processes in my life, which led to a continual cycle of sexual addiction over forty years. But just two years ago, I experienced something wonderful"

As an eleven year old boy I was faced with something that no child should ever be confronted with – I was being asked to expose myself to my teacher. His request came as a shock, but he qualified it with words that have become so cheap in our society, "I love you." My family didn't talk much about love, in fact my father was a very aggressive man, more prone to giving me a beating than a hug.

Therefore, when my teacher said how he loved me, I was intrigued, and over the next four years he educated me in all the things that he wanted to do to me. He made me class librarian to ensure he had plenty of time with me privately, as he tried to persuade me to expose myself to him. He made it all seem so nice; but fearing God, and what would happen if I did give in, enabled me to keep my trousers on.

However, after four years my mind was filled with all kinds of imagery and thoughts. Nothing could control the desires that began to come to the surface. At night, after another cruel beating by my Father, I would go to bed and think about my teacher and how, "he loved me." Throughout my teenage years I fantasized about being touched by a man; I wanted the warmth and the love of a man's embrace, as the only man that I really knew was my father, but he didn't love me, he never affirmed me, never spoke kindly to me - rather he vented his anger on me. So I despised him.

Through my teenage years, I was eaten by the desire for my school teacher, but my strong evangelical background meant I could never do the things he asked, as God would surely strike me dead or else damn me to hell. To deal with my despair, I developed a fantasy world that always culminated in masturbation. It was a world that I was trapped in; nothing could deliver me out of it. I was a secret homosexual, and listening to adult evangelical conversation confirmed I was a pervert. I tried Christianity, making a profession early in life, which I renewed when I was about eighteen. I went to Bible College and was ordained a minister. I got married and have three beautiful children, but none of these things could remove the desires, created in my mind by my school teacher, that cried out for expression.

Sexual relations with another man didn't really happen until I was in my forties. Yes, there were a couple of minor incidents in my teenage years, but it was after a mental breakdown that things changed. The main factors that led to my breakdown were that I couldn't maintain a spiritual walk with God with all that was in my head. My marriage grew more and more difficult; I loved my wife, but we had many issues. In a way, my wife replaced my father. She didn't beat me up physically, but mentally she tortured me. Further pressure came from the elders of the church where I served as minister. I ended up being consigned to a mental hospital, drugged on anti-depressants, wanting to commit suicide. Life was over for me, I was a reject - and all because I allowed the thoughts implanted in my mind when I was eleven to take a grip of my soul. My father, my wife, my church, my sin - everything had conspired and made an end of me. My only hope was suicide. Hopefully, God would hear my prayer before I could end my life, and my children would forgive me because I was ill. Tortured, I was to blame. I was useless - my father always told me that. I wasn't the person my elders wanted, even though I had the support of the people. I wasn't the husband my wife wanted - she continually reminded me of the more worthy men she could have married. I was doomed!

But thankfully, after three years of gradual recovery, I finally came out the other side. After much heart searching during those dark years, with Bible study, prayer and support by many loving Christians, I emerged. But I emerged a different person; my marriage was over, the church had failed me, and I was a confirmed homosexual destined to live happily ever after.

Looking back today, I am sorry that my marriage ended as it did, with my involvement in homosexuality. It started with me cruising for casual sex with men, developing rapidly to picking up men daily and sometimes several times a day. With my wife gone, I could bring them back to my home for sex. Next, looking for love, I launched into a series of relationships; but of course I never found it, only more bondage, lies and heartache. My desires became addictive, to the point that I felt I had become an unpaid male prostitute. At the merest hint of suggestion, I was engaging in every aspect of homosexual depravity. I was everybody's friend, but afterwards left lonely and used. I really thought I was living. Medically, I had been told I would never work again as a result of my breakdown, but here I was with a new professional career in education. God hadn't struck me dead, I was fine. But in fact everything was not rosy! Equating homosexual practice with happiness, i.e. "GAY", is anything but the truth.

My homosexuality was the result of serious dysfunctional processes in my life which led to a continual cycle of sexual addiction over forty years. But just two years ago, I experienced something wonderful - the presence of God's Holy Spirit calling me to repentance and deliverance. At first I mocked the idea of experiencing change. But I was directed to Matthew 11:28, where Jesus says, "Come to me, all of you who are tired and have heavy loads." That certainly was very appropriate to how I was feeling, but Jesus goes on to say, "I will give you rest." How marvellous is that! I so wanted rest, the cycle of sexual addiction had turned into utter bondage. The gay lifestyle is all about meeting an ever wider circle of men, whose agenda is about exploring the depths of human depravity. The world of a gay man is not about meeting other gay men to have a drink and socialize, it is about seeking a bigger fix next time for your sexual ego.

But I had had enough. I was extremely unhappy. 'Friendship' could only be obtained in the circle of gay networks that exist, where they are targeted towards meeting a particular 'bondage'. However, the Holy Spirit was pointing me to a friendship that was based not on bondage, but on deliverance. In 2 Corinthians 5:21 we read, "Christ had no sin, but God made Him become sin, so that in Christ we could become right with God." Being, "right with God" is where the change begins, and God is the one who creates the change. Paul emphasises that Christ, who was sinless, was made to be a sex addict for me, so that I might become sexually pure before God. What wonderful freedom Christ purchased for us in His death!

Over the past two years, I have been beginning to experience that freedom as I learn more of the grace of God, something that was so foreign to me in my previous experience of Christianity. Every day I am experiencing change in my thoughts, in my actions. As I bring my brokenness to the Cross, I experience grace sufficient for every need. This is not a popular message to those who are in the grip of dysfunction; it didn't grip me much, either. I have protested against it and raised my gay pride expertise about it, but to no avail. In John 8:36 we read, "So if the Son makes you free, you will be truly free." Only as the Spirit of God makes this truth a reality, will you experience this freedom.

Let me be truthful – there have been many times of victory, but I have also had discouragements. Yet I am so thankful that I belong to a church fellowship that understands my struggle. As well as my helpful pastor, one of the elders acts as an accountability partner for me. He listens and encourages me to keep pressing ahead.

Also, a professional Christian counsellor has inspired me to address the hurts in my past. This safe, confidential environment enables me to speak without fear. Biblical passages remind me that all things are possible to those who trust in Christ's redemptive work.

I know that this message will meet resistance from some. But I must proclaim the radical message of the Cross. Jesus said, "In this world you will have trouble, but be brave, I have defeated the world." Whatever your bondage, Christ has defeated it.

Jacob: Choosing to align my sexuality with my spirituality

"I don't want to be pushed in any direction, but one thing I know right now is that embracing homosexuality is not consistent with my faith. To be told that I should therefore change my faith to allow homosexual practice makes no sense to me at all."

I first remember feeling different from around the age of 5 or 6. I look back now and wonder if my parents had any inkling when I asked if it would be okay to wear a pink bow-tie for the family photo (I still have the photo)! It just seemed I was so different from my older brother, our interests were worlds apart. He let me know from an early age that there were certain names for boys who liked to read, and paint, and do gymnastics rather than play football - "fruit", "poof", "sissy". I remember the acute pain that those names brought to me.

The home in which we were raised was a troubled one. My father worked two jobs, the second one being part-time with the army. In spite of the fact that he provided for us well materially, he was distant emotionally, often critical and argumentative, and was drunk almost every weekend. He and my mother fought constantly, and very often he left her with bruises and blackened eyes, on one occasion even hospitalising her. She in turn became very depressed, and sometimes spoke openly about her desire to die. I think in many ways, being a sensitive boy who loved his mother dearly, I became an emotional crutch for my mum, and she would confide in me, and look to me for comfort and support. She criticised my father to me, and as time went on I grew more and more detached from him and made an inner decision that I never wanted to be like him.

After being sexualised early by an older boy, I quickly became aware of feelings of guilt and shame. I recall one occasion when staying at a friend's house overnight, we kissed and touched each other, and in the morning I made a promise to God that it would never happen again. It happened several times after that. Into early adolescence, I became a very quiet and shy individual, with very little confidence. I retreated into the world of reading, and excelled academically at school. While I was very capable athletically, I lacked the confidence of the other boys, and therefore mostly tended to remain detached and uninvolved. Soon it seemed like others who were also considered "unacceptable" and different to the norm had 'found' each other, and we became a group of friends in which it was okay to be unique and expressive. One or two of the lads in the group were quite effeminate and flamboyant, and I was hugely drawn to their sense of humour and fun. At this time, my identity confusion was growing, and while I dated several girls, I never felt entirely comfortable and was increasingly feeling attractions for my own gender.

While not brought up in a Christian home, I always had a belief in God and an awareness that I was accountable to him. Having been invited to an evangelistic campaign in a small Pentecostal mission, for the first time I was confronted by the claims of the gospel and, at the age of 17, accepted Christ into my life as Lord and Saviour. Almost overnight I fell in love with God and his people, and the direction of my life was changed completely. I experienced a joy and a peace that I had never known before, and gradually with time, began to experience real change in many areas of my life, including my relationships to my parents. However, this issue about my sexuality was something which continued to bother me. I struggled with it alone in silence, never daring to share what it was I was feeling, since the only message I ever heard about it from the church was quite negative.

One day I stumbled upon a little tract, "Dear Robert", describing the change someone had experienced in moving successfully away from a gay lifestyle. I must have read and re-read it over a hundred times! As I studied God's word, I couldn't get round the fact that the Bible describes homosexual practice as sin. I knew that it wasn't in His will for my life, and yet I felt deeply conflicted between the desire to please Him, and the desire to please my own flesh. I've come to realise this is not a battle unique to one wrestling with homosexual desires, but one common to every Christian. The call of Christ is to deny ourselves, take up the cross and follow Him.

Looking up the website on this booklet opened to me a world that I never before knew existed – the "ex-gay" world. As I read more and more, I made discoveries about myself (often painfully), and could identify the roots from which my feelings had sprung. Although I continued to fight alone for the next few years, several hurtful experiences of emotional dependency with other older men finally made me realise I needed to seek out help in order to find space in my thinking about what I really wanted. For me the issue was a clear matter of authority – either I would follow Christ, and allow His word to chart the course of my life, or I would be my own lord and follow the dictates of my own heart.

I was so thankful to find a Christian counsellor who understood and empathised with my situation. Recognising the value-base to which I held, he supported me in my choice to voluntarily attempt to move away from a same-sex attracted orientation. What a relief it was to be able to share openly and freely with others who could identify with the same desire to please God over and above the pull of homosexual attraction. Proverbs 27:19 says, "As in water, face answers to face, so the heart of man to man". Giving and receiving, being open and transparent in this setting, felt like having a bucket dropped down into the deep well of my heart, pulled out and its contents being splashed around for me to finally see. Simultaneously, God gave me opportunities to share my struggle with some in my church family, and their response of love and encouragement was overwhelming.

As I have continued to walk in this path, it has not always been easy. There have been, and continue to be, times of real struggle and difficulty, and listening to that one Voice in the midst of a multitude that clamour for my attention is a challenge indeed. But I'm thankful that in spite of the struggle that remains, I do not need to be either controlled or defined by it. My identity is not in sexuality or in a label the world would want to give me, but in who I am in Christ. On my journey with Him, He continues to reveal to me His unconditional love and new depths of His grace, and when I fail, it is His goodness that leads me to repentance. I know that He is a jealous God who consistently calls me to surrender to His claims of lordship over my life, trusting that His ways are good and best for me. In this past year, He has been challenging many of my comfort zones, and patiently showing me that true courage is not the absence of fear, but action in the face of fear. Although as of yet I am not dating, the desire of my heart is to press on to all that He has for me, to continue to grow in Him and experience the sufficiency of His grace, which has brought me safe thus far, and will lead me safely home.

A prayer to the God of the ebb and flow:

Dear Lord, today I thought of the words of Vincent Van Gogh, "It is true that there is an ebb and flow, but the sea remains the sea". You are the sea. Although I experience many ups and downs in my emotions, and often feel great shifts and changes in my inner life, you remain the same. Your sameness is not the sameness of a rock, but the sameness of a faithful lover. Out of your love I came to life; by your love I am sustained; and to your love I am always called back. There are days of sadness and days of joy; there are feelings of guilt and feelings of gratitude; there are moments of failure and moments of success; but all of them are embraced by your unwavering love. My only real temptation is to doubt your love, to think of myself as beyond the reach of your love, to remove myself from the healing radiance of your love. To do these things is to move into the darkness of despair. O Lord, sea of love and goodness, let me not fear too much the storms and winds of daily life, and let me know that there is ebb and flow, but that the sea remains the sea. Amen".

Samuel: Reflections of a changed and grateful traveller

"Certain bodies are lobbying for an end to therapy for men who want to overcome these struggles. How dare they! As a man who has been on the receiving end of it, and a medical professional myself, I say we should give it greater support."

"I shall be telling this with a sigh, Somewhere ages and ages hence:
Two roads diverged in a wood, and I -- I took the one less travelled by,
And that has made all the difference." Robert Frost

When I was asked to write something about my journey, I thought it would be easy. Surely something that I have faced, struggled, and battled with for years should be easy to put into words. It wasn't, and I spent days avoiding it. With reflection on what has gone before, here, finally, is my story.

My journey to change started in the summer of 2008, when I made an effort to find someone who could help me. I had been aware of my struggle with same-sex attraction for a number of years, but it had become more pronounced in my late teens and as I started university. Living a homosexually orientated lifestyle was not something I wanted. It went against my Christian beliefs, and it did not allow for the wife and family that I longed for when I was older.

One afternoon in August, I had a meeting with a man who was experienced in this field and, for the first time sharing with anyone, I opened up about my life and the struggles I faced. It was an emotional meeting. Something I had kept to myself for so many years, I suddenly made known to a man I had never met before. It all came out, along with the tears and heartache. He did a lot of listening, but he also told me that I wasn't alone. That there were many men who struggled with these attractions and who, like me, wanted nothing to do with them. I was encouraged. He told me that some of these men found it useful to talk with people about their struggles in an attempt to better understand. This was one thing I wanted - better understanding. Why did I, a young man who grew up in a Christian home, who wanted nothing more than to be in a loving heterosexual relationship, have these attractions?

I was then put in contact with a therapist who had particular expertise that was relevant to my needs. Over the next eighteen months, I met with him fairly regularly. I explained my struggles and that it was not the way in which I wanted to live my life. I wanted to change. We looked at different aspects of my life: my friends, family, my past. It helped me to better understand why I was the person I was. I could see that for a lot of my life, although I was never a loner and had a loving father, I did lack a strong male influence, with my mother taking a leading role in caring for my brother and me.

After a few months, the therapist suggested I join a group that he ran, of men who like myself struggled with same-sex attraction, but did not want to live a homosexual lifestyle. For the first time, I met others who were going through the very same thing I had battled with for so long. Men from all sorts of backgrounds, all of whom shared a common struggle. The group met every two weeks, and was a safe place in which we could share the things on our hearts, and together could help one another deal with the hardships we faced.

Over three years later, I am a different man. Being part of the men's group has given me an immense understanding around the issue of same-sex attraction, but more importantly has shown me why I might struggle and how I might better meet the needs in my life, which if left unattended can often make things worse. I came to realise that close male friendships were something I was lacking. I brought this before God, asking him to provide me with men who would love and encourage me. How he answered that prayer! I moved in to share a house with several guys, and embarked on friendships which I have no doubt helped to build me up into the man I am today – more confident and assured of my masculinity and worth. I now realise that authentic relationships with other men were something I lacked, and are now proving a great blessing in my life.

However, does meeting a therapist, attending a group, and having good friends mean that I don't struggle with same-sex attraction anymore? No. It's still an issue in my life, and one which I've come to accept might not fully go away, but it has certainly lessened. I can now say it is not my identity and it doesn't have to determine my life. Last year I entered into a relationship with a woman, something I was never confident to do before. I could never have imagined that before I began on this journey. Although that relationship has now ended, I can see that a heterosexual relationship is something I am capable of having, and excited to have again.

Often I wonder what my life would be like now if I hadn't made that effort to seek help four years ago. I hope that I would still have been fighting the struggle against same-sex attraction and avoiding the temptation of that sort of lifestyle – but how much more difficult that fight would be! Therapy has allowed me to understand better the battle I face. It has empowered me, and given me the encouragement I need, as I share with other people who have the same issues. I have met people who live with these attractions, some of whom have been in homosexual relationships and others who haven't, but who are now married and have children. There is hope!

Certain bodies are lobbying for an end to therapy for men who want to overcome these struggles. How dare they! As a man who has been on the receiving end of this kind of help, and a medical professional myself, I say we should give it greater support. There are many men in my position, who are looking for the support offered by therapists and support groups currently under attack. It is surely at the discretion of the one reaching out for that support, whether or not to avail themselves of it. Why should they be denied such a lifeline?

I am eternally thankful for the support I have received through therapy, and for the men in the group who have been integral in the change I have seen in my life. Although I may have taken the road less travelled, I was not alone. They were there, walking alongside me.

David and Sophie: A happily married couple

"I love David with all my heart and I am truly blessed to have him as my husband."

'I now pronounce you husband and wife. You may kiss the bride'

These are familiar words for most of us, although for me they were words which, at times in my life, I never thought would be spoken directly to me. So when that moment finally arrived, it was an extra special milestone in my journey.

From a very young age I felt 'different' from many of the other boys I used to play with. I always seemed to be more comfortable around other males. When I hit puberty, I was definitely very aware that I was attracted mainly to other guys, although not exclusively. I was rather scared of women, and the thought of doing anything physical with one just didn't appeal at all.

I became a Christian around this time and I knew that being an active homosexual wasn't part of God's plan for me. As I grew older, the attraction for men remained, although I never acted on it despite being tempted many times. The scariest thing for me during this period, wasn't that I was a gay living secretly in a Christian world, but that I felt that I had no alternative but to act on these attractions. Society told me that I was repressing my desires and I should just go with the flow. However, I just couldn't do it.

During a meal with some old university friends, one of them mentioned a guy we all knew from university days. Apparently this guy was getting married to a woman! Nothing remarkable there you might think, but this guy had been living a gay lifestyle at university. The other remarkable thing was that this guy didn't, and as far as I know doesn't, have any religious beliefs.

I realized that if this guy was able to move away from his lifestyle and get married, then there was no reason that I couldn't too. It gave me some hope, but I promised myself I would never ever get married just for the sake of it. Although I wanted to so much, I just knew it would be selfish and unfair to get married to a girl if there was no love or attraction there. If that meant that I was going to be single and celibate forever, then so be it!

A few years and a few failed relationships later, and I was still no further forward, but I knew there was something missing in my life. The attraction for other men was still there too. However, things were about to change.

I agreed to meet Sophie on a blind date after a few gentle nudges from some mutual friends. We had a great first date, and after three hours of coffee and cakes we were still chatting. A few dates later, and we decided we would become an item and give a relationship a go. This was great, and as the weeks passed by I was beginning to fall for her. We just got on so well and, even though we had different personalities, we seemed to work well together. However, I was uneasy; the other promise I had made to myself was if I ever met a girl and there was a chance this might work out, I would need to tell her about myself. No secrets.

I'll let Sophie continue the story…

I remember there were times in my life when I wanted to know what the future would be like – I wanted to know all the answers to my big questions. However, as I have travelled though my Christian journey, I have realized the blessing of not knowing, as the Lord is preparing our hearts for what He has planned. It is amazing to look back through my journey so far, and see how the Lord was preparing me to meet David before I ever knew him. Sometimes I wonder what it would've been like to have met him sooner, but then I am reminded that our lives and hearts were not at that point ready.

There are two key incidents that I can reflect on where God challenged my thinking on homosexuality. I went to an event in a church about relationships, and there was a panel of Christians with a variety of relationship experiences – married, single, and someone who had lived a gay lifestyle before becoming a Christian. I was amazed at their stories, and how what they said answered many questions I had. The point they made that has stuck with me, is how the world emphasizes the importance of sexual relationships and neglects the importance of friendships. The point was raised that while the world wants our young people to obsess about having boyfriends and girlfriends, we should be encouraging them to build friendships.

Around the same time as this event, I was increasingly concerned that my mum was depressed and had something on her mind. We went for a walk one evening and she cried her heart out. She wouldn't tell me what was wrong, just that I would find out soon. After talking to her and comforting her, I learned that during the holidays my sister had told her she was gay. My mum had confided in my dad. They both loved their daughter deeply, but didn't know how to deal with this information and, with my sister living away from home, it wasn't easy for them to talk to her. I had already planned a trip to see my sister. We were very close and it was hard for me to get my head around things too, but I wanted to let her know how much I loved her and would always love her.

I started to see people differently, especially guys I dated, as in the back of my mind was the question, 'How will you react if I have to tell you about my sister someday?' Every time I heard someone make a joke about being gay, I felt like I was being kicked in the stomach. I loved my sister and I knew I couldn't be with someone who was ignorant and obnoxious.

And then I met David and, cheesy as it sounds, I remember thinking 'where have you been all my life?' Our lives just clicked into place, it confirmed to me that God's timing is always perfect. I knew there would come a day when I would have to tell him about my sister. I knew I was falling in love with him, and that I would have to tell him soon - so I did and I remember him saying that it wouldn't make a difference on how he saw or treated her.

One evening after we had dinner at David's house, I remember he said he needed to tell me something. David said I could leave if I wanted once he told me, but it was something I needed to know before our relationship continued any further. Then he referred to my sister, and said he understood how she feels because he has known those same struggles himself. I just remember holding him and telling him I wasn't going anywhere.

I have such admiration and respect for David, for his strength of character, his patience and his faith in the Lord. I love him with all my heart and I am truly blessed to have him as my husband…

So that's our story. We look forward to many more happy years in our journey through life together.

Simon: My experience of therapy

"When I feel the connectedness to other men in terms of mutually expressed non-sexual affections – which I missed as a boy – I feel masculine inside and lose my sexual inclinations towards men. Reparative Therapy has provided me with real hope ..."

The therapy that I have received is known as Reparative Therapy (RT). Although the term is often used in a general sense to describe any attempt to reduce same-sex attraction, RT itself is a specific type of therapy. Given the many popular views propagated by the media, which often gravely distort or exaggerate what is actually involved, I thought it might be helpful if I say what this therapy is, and what it is not.

It is a 'talking therapy' and doesn't involve electric shocks. In fact, all my sessions were conducted by telephone. The therapist explores with the client their 'body states' experienced in connection with particular feelings being felt, and the accompanying experiences connected to important episodes in daily life. One of the main 'body states' the therapist looked at with me, was when feelings of shame were felt in the body and how this was symptomatic of not being in an emotionally assertive and truly relaxed state that naturally embodies my masculinity (i.e. at ease with myself in terms of my body and my place in the world, especially among heterosexual men, but also in terms of how I perceive women.)

RT involves neither repressing sexual feelings, nor any kind of 'trying' to be interested in the opposite sex, but rather learning to connect with men as brothers, along with developing an unconditional self-acceptance. If and when changes in sexual orientation occur, they *flow naturally as a consequence* of work in connection with overcoming shame issues around men, and feelings of 'not fitting in' with men and one's place in their world as equals.

What made me want to receive RT? The RT was not religious in any way. However, the therapist was happy to hear me discuss aspects of my Christian faith as and when they arose. I entered RT hoping to develop my heterosexual potential. My same-sex attractions began in early adolescence, but I did not want to practise homosexuality. For me, sexual relations find meaningful expression in marriage between a man and a woman. I also knew that there were a number of markers in my upbringing that I believe led to my homosexual feelings in the first place.

At school I didn't like sport and never felt like 'one of the boys'. I experienced some trauma from bullying and name-calling. I had few friends and felt more at home with adults, but only on an emotionally superficial level.

RT has repeatedly corroborated the experiences of my upbringing. Books on RT read like my biography. So RT felt like the most natural and desirable course, offering me the prospect of letting go of something (homosexuality) that brought me huge unhappiness. I could never have found happiness in the gay world. In 1997 I began RT, with sessions every two or three weeks. I continued my engineering studies, supported by a part-time job.

For many years I had had a negative view of women. I also felt fear of being controlled by a woman. In my teens, every young woman reminded me of my older sister, who held a controlling and disapproving influence over me which I hated. I could see my sister's disapproving face overlaid on their faces. So I disliked (not hated) women and had no emotional or sexual interest in them. When I passed young men on the street, I had a feeling of terror and couldn't make eye contact with them. Through pornography my attraction to men became more sexual and compulsive. I became increasingly depressed. There was no religion in my home, but I began to experience the Christian faith in my late twenties. Before entering RT, I began making friends with other men in church. For the first time, I felt respected by my peers even when they knew about my same-sex attractions. When I changed churches (for unrelated reasons), however, I felt unable to find similar support.

I always felt 'let down' by the medical profession because, while officially therapists say they will not judge the client, they would not accept the validity of my choice not to identify as gay. I felt angry, cheated and discriminated against. The consultations contradicted the principle of self-determination that I was promised. I felt I had to defend myself and explain my position, and felt isolated and unsupported. I discovered that no professional in the UK, if they followed official guidelines, could unconditionally respect my values. This caused me deep upset and pain that words cannot express.

My RT therapist encouraged me to understand what was behind my same-sex attractions. When I felt shame, my body would enter a less assertive state, and this would be a warning sign that predisposed me to fantasise and act out with masturbation and pornography. Before RT, I rarely felt able to expose my vulnerabilities with men. RT helped me realise that I wasn't getting my legitimate (non-sexual) needs met, because of my barrier of shame. But enabled to feel free of these feelings - through RT - I found that the compulsive sexual yearnings for men would lose their power. As I learned to connect with once-feared men, I was amazed to find that they also reached out to me and my attractions weakened.

When I feel connectedness to other men in terms of mutually expressed non-sexual affections – which I missed as a boy – I feel masculine inside and lose my sexual inclinations towards men. RT has provided me with real hope, and has demystified the issue of my needs around my male peers. I am not 'different' from other men, but their equal.

I no longer see women as like my older sister. I appreciate femininity in a new way. When I am at peace with my own body (no shame) I can be physically attracted to women. While I still have much to learn about the opposite sex, without the insights I learned from RT, these prospects would be nil.

I have experienced the joy of brotherhood with all men. I belong to their world and no longer feel 'on the outside'. RT has taught me that same-sex attractions are built on unmet needs and childhood-derived hurts, and that without the triggering experiences of shame there is no homosexuality left. This discovery corroborates my belief that it makes no sense to stake ownership on an identity ('being gay') whose foundations are incompatible with the experiences I've had of healthy, shame-free manhood.

Stephen: Jumping ship from sexual confusion to a fulfilling life

"I hope and pray that if you see yourself in this story, you will find some consolation and that there are answers to your needs, confusions and struggles."

I grew up in West Belfast, the youngest of six children, in a catholic community as a child of the troubles. My family had nationalist / republican leanings. My dad sang in a folk group and our house was always being raided by the police and British army. He was quite an absent father for most of my life for many reasons. My mum's and his relationship had been shaky for years. Though I was the youngest, I felt the tension in the house, with little display of affection between them.

One day, one of the girls in my street, who was about three years older than me (and I was only eight or nine), wanted to show me something - what sex was. She asked me to try it with her. I did and the experience was explosive; being so young I did not know what to do with such a powerful thing. It led me down a very dark road that causes me lots of guilt and shame. We subsequently did it a number of times, and I wanted it more and more. Masturbation became part of my daily routine, and my fantasy life started developing beyond normal appropriate boundaries.

When I hit puberty, things shifted up a gear. One day two boys, my closest friends, mimed a sexual act with each other to my horror. I was disturbed by the idea as I knew how sex was meant to work. I remember thinking this is wrong and yet for days after I thought about it – that guys could pleasure each other. This culminated in me masturbating with another close friend. I felt ashamed and guilty. I ended the friendship, as I couldn't face my friend after this. My fantasy included heterosexual thoughts and feelings as well as homosexual ones. I was mainly still attracted to girls but sometimes troubled with homosexual thoughts.

Rather than paint a picture that is all doom and gloom and leaves out some of the good things in my life, let me list here some moments of love and nurturing that filled my heart and redressed the balance. My first confession with Fr Murphy - I always liked his smile. My mum running her fingers through my hair. My dad asking me to take the day off school to go to the motor show. New Year's Eve parties in our house, where our friends came to drink and be merry. Playing Malone Inner Nine with dad's Bobby Locke clubs. Years on my BMX that I bought with my paper run money. Trench house forest, where I would climb trees and try to get chased by the gardener. Learning to canoe and doing Eskimo rolls. Teachers who showed genuine concern and affection.

Life was not all bad, but the corroding effects of a dysfunctional family, conflicts with peers and a community in conflict with itself, coupled with some powerful secretive sexual experiences when I was far too young to understand, didn't create in me a mental and emotional sense of wellbeing. I just couldn't hold a secure grip on life. It was like having a bucket of water that just leaked out through the holes.

Into this foray, one of my friends invited me to our local catholic parish, to a youth mission / outreach. The relationships I made through this group changed my world. The contrast between this new group and my existing friends couldn't have been starker. They lived by a set of values which I had not previously seen lived in my own wee world. They had happily married families, and were able to resolve conflicts within themselves amicably. The way they expressed their love didn't involve sex outside marriage, and their sense of community was intoxicating. They were also a bunch of Catholics and Protestants running this mission, which in 1989 in West Belfast was very risky. They had a type of faith that was more experiential and real than any I had encountered. I'm not saying they were perfect, but they were much better than anything I had ever seen.

At this time, I was partying in the gay scene and getting drunk every weekend. I had been having sex with girls when I got the opportunity. My new friends didn't believe this was right. It never felt like they were condemning me, but I slowly became convinced. There was authority and power in their lives – a governing authority founded on a relationship with God, plus a family and community authority, as their lives were so much healthier and more functional - yet they didn't brag or boast as if this was so.

For months I lived in two different worlds. My partying and hedonistic/nihilistic community, and another community who lived from Christian values. I watched as some of my friends in the party scene got STI's, and one died from HIV. In one community we lived reckless high-risk life styles, while the other was shaped to protect and nurture personal wellbeing. It didn't take long for me to jump ship. I completely left the party scene. I just couldn't get enough of this Christian community – they had something I intuitively knew was nurturing me, and along with this came some profound spiritual experience that can only be described as catalytic and transformative.

Over the next seven years I became less self-absorbed. I went from very poor sexual self-control to learning how to curb my appetites. I went from masturbating a number of times a day, to gaps of months to over a year. I slowly got clean of most of my sexual dreams and erotic fantasy life. This was in part due to being caught up in something bigger than me, a higher power – Jesus, youth and community work. My mind filled up with other more interesting things than just my confused sexual explorations of where I'd been, looking for love in all the wrong places. As I got my emotional, mental and spiritual needs met in a loving Christian community, I didn't need to go to sex as a substitute for love. I realized it never was intended to resolve all our deepest needs, it was meant to be an expression of love, not an expression of need.

Later, after a seven long years of living a chaste lifestyle, where self-control and abstinence was esteemed, I found my needs for affirmation and affection were being met and my cravings dissipated. I started for the first time to date - out of desire and purpose, and not out of need. This made all the difference in attracting someone who was strong and healthy, where before I attracted people just as needy as myself.

I have been married for fourteen years now and have four children, and one on the way. I went back to university as a mature student and got a degree. I have been running a successful non-profit organisation that my wife and I founded. I feel we have to pass on what we have learnt: share, teach and train others in the skills and character development we pick up on the way.

I would never say I have it all together, but when I look back on my life and that wee eight year old kid, and see the transformation and the complications I had to overcome, it was all worth it. I hope and pray that, if you see yourself in this story, you will find some consolation and that there are answers to your needs, confusions and struggles. First, get established in a loving community, with a high value for your wellbeing and an ability to mentor you as you walk through the process to recovery and freedom. And, if you are merciful to yourself and can let the love in, you will see a miracle that you never thought possible. May the Lord bless you and keep you all the days of your life.

James: A journey 'beyond gay'

"I am deeply grateful to the unwavering commitment, courage and witness manifested to me through a whole network of outstanding men and women who dared to believe in me against all odds, especially the long-suffering therapists."

I grew up believing myself to have been born gay. Why should I think otherwise? I had always, and only, had the most powerful, all-consuming, erotic attraction towards my own sex since early childhood, and came out to my family, friends and at school when I was seventeen years old. At eighteen I moved to London from the North of England and more fully embraced my gay identity. At university, I was a key person in helping to establish a lesbian and gay group. I was very much out and proud - wholeheartedly and pro-actively gay.

I saw my mission in life as serving the gay community and preaching its activist messages. Because of my Christian upbringing and my desire to know more about God, I went along regularly to the meetings of the *Lesbian and Gay Christian Movement*. I learnt a lot about safe sex at that time – but not a lot about the Gospel! For a time I was very promiscuous, but then settled down with a long-term boyfriend, and we considered travelling abroad at that time to enter into a civil partnership together, such was our commitment to one another.

I came into a committed relationship with Jesus Christ around this time, and began to examine my life more deeply. I came to realize that I had some unresolved issues relating to childhood events. I sought healing prayer from other Christians, in the power of the Holy Spirit, to help me find resolution in areas where I needed to learn to forgive – and I had many people, especially men, from my past that I needed to forgive.

As I found resolution for past wounds, changes began to take place in the way I saw myself, my relationships, and even my sexual orientation. I had never thought about "changing orientation". Why should I need to? I believed myself to be born gay and didn't believe in "change". However, when through prayer and therapy my voice began to grow deeper, and my effeminate walk became more deliberate and masculine - and, as the healing prayer and great therapy with trained professionals took deeper root within me - I came, slowly at first, to the realization that my core identity could not, indeed *must not*, be restricted and minimized by words relating to sexual orientation. To do this would be to dishonour myself and God's ability to work in my life. I reached a point where I had to either totally reject everything to do with 'being gay', or remain stuck and unable to move forward into true manhood, which has always been my greatest inheritance from God.

I embarked upon cognitive therapy to focus on specific problems, behavioural therapy to change problematic actions that had been trained through years of reinforcement, group therapy, EMDR, and finally psychoanalytic therapy - all enshrouded in healing prayer, and with the support of a great new community around me, who believed there was a "true man" created by God within the core of my person.

I had envisaged myself spending my entire life preaching that people are born gay, and for those who do not understand homosexuality to, "get over it – and quick" ("bigoted, intolerant, ill-educated lot" is what I thought of them). The total opposite, however, has become true. After intensive therapy for three years during my early twenties, a whole new aspect of my very "self" began to rise up, a part of "me" that I never knew existed, that I had never discovered and embraced, but what I would now term as "the true man". I had not expected or planned for this to happen. Why should I, when I never thought I could or should be any different to who I was? After all I was born gay, wasn't I? Or was I…?

I came to a place where I realized that, although I had made the courageous and painful journey to come wholly "out" as a gay man, there was in fact another infinitely more important and significant journey that I needed to take - one that would bring an inner peace I had never experienced before, yet had often glimpsed and, yes, found deeply attractive (and been slightly jealous of), in heterosexual men. It is a journey I see so many same-sex attracted men and women yearning to take, but they are led to look for the route in the wrong places. The majority either don't know how, or, as is the case more recently, are being denied the opportunity to take this journey. As was true for me, I see clearly now that the vast majority of same-sex attracted people have been hoodwinked into believing that gay affirmation will bring peace – which of course it does quite dramatically for a time, as a by-product of accepting the reality of their present situation. This same limiting journey of gay affirmation requires that a demand is made for everything that other-sex attracted people have, such as children and marriage. And yet, even with full access to these, there will not - because there cannot - be true rest deep within the same-sex attracted person, because at the very core of each person's spirit is the need for strong gender affirmation, and the same-sex attracted person needs copious amounts of this, even more than other-sex attracted people.

Five years after intensive therapy, I began to see my now ex-boyfriend for who he really was: an amazing man, but someone deeply unaffirmed in the core of his masculine identity. He, however, could not move beyond seeing me as an object of his erotic desire and found it impossible, even abhorrent, trying to embark upon a chaste friendship with me. And so any possibility of true friendship died.

I took the therapeutic journey that demanded leaving no stone unturned, and ended up living among men and women in a way I would never have done if I had remained "encased" in the gay community, or in a gay identity. My 'ex', who had been a strapping masculine, medalled soldier when I met him, had tragically become an effeminate, HIV ridden, and lonely man within the space of these few years. I knew more than ever that my decision to embark on therapy, and especially that which concentrates on repairing malformed sexual orientation, saved my life in the long run (and saved a lot of taxpayers' money too!).

I am deeply grateful to the unwavering commitment, courage and witness manifested to me through a whole network of outstanding men and women, who dared to believe in me against all odds; especially the long-suffering therapists. Without their encouragement - and there were *many* who discouraged me, especially from within the "gay ranks", and within the so-called Christian church - I would never be married today with a family. I would also never have been able to reach out in support of the literally hundreds of deeply courageous, same-sex attracted men and women who have walked, and continue to walk, a similar journey to my own.

EPILOGUE - The Right to Decide

"The individual has the right to choose whether he or she wishes to become straight. It is his or her choice, not that of an ideologically driven interest group. To discourage a psychotherapist from undertaking a client wishing to convert ... [is] anti-research, anti-scholarship, and antithetical toward the quest for truth."[2]

Robert Perloff, former President, American Psychological Association

The stories told in the foregoing pages reflect the lives of people who have struggled to rid themselves of unwanted attractions to members of the same sex. It is striking that, despite what they have so often been told, many of them do not believe that they were 'born that way', much less that 'God made them that way.' Neither, obviously, did they 'choose to be that way'. Could there be another pathway into homosexuality that is neither biologically predetermined nor freely chosen?

It is tragically clear that a disproportionate number of our storytellers experienced some form of sexual abuse during childhood, and that these individuals attribute their subsequent difficulties in achieving normal heterosexual adjustment at least in part to this violation of their childhood innocence. Others report a difficult relationship with the same-sex parent - the father in this case, because most of the storytellers are men – and sometimes a corresponding over-attachment to their mother. It is possible that for these people (though not necessarily for *most* people) those relationships may have been a contributory factor to their sexuality.

Peer group rejection may be another causal factor – one respondent describes graphically (what may have been the experience to a lesser degree for some others) how, following prolonged illness, he was rejected by the boys in school and had to play with the girls. Who could measure the pain of such rejection, or deny its potential for long term consequences?

All of this is consistent with what science has found – that environmental factors specific to each individual person early in life may be influential in shaping sexual orientation. This is shown most clearly in twin studies, which suggest that genes and hormones exert only a minor effect in causing same-sex attractions; if this is correct, early life experiences are likely to be the main causal influences.

---

2 http://narth.com/docs/perloff.html <09 August, 2012>

Yet the scientific establishment (which seems to change direction on this issue every few decades) currently denies that this is so. The Royal College of Psychiatrists, for example, says, "It would appear that sexual orientation is biological in nature, determined by genetic factors and/or the early uterine environment."[3] Their discussion, however, doesn't even mention twin studies, which have been central to the scientific research in recent years. This omission is a gaping hole which seriously undermines the persuasiveness of the Royal College's argument.

It is extraordinary that the Royal College should deliberately ignore such a fundamental category of evidence. Why would they do this? A plausible explanation is that twin studies research challenges today's dominant ideology, which seeks to promote the view that homosexuality is biologically determined and fixed, and that it can't be changed any more than can the colour of one's skin. The logic of this ideology is that it would be unethical for a therapist to assist a person seeking to move away from same-sex attraction. This is in fact the line that has been followed by the mental health guilds in the UK.

Thus the UK Council for Psychotherapy bans therapists from all attempts to reduce same-sex attraction, saying that, "There is overwhelming evidence that undergoing such therapy is at considerable emotional and psychological cost"[4] – though it offers no credible evidence for this assertion.

The consequences of this dogmatic stance are dramatic for people such as those represented in this book. Such people are alarmed that the lifeline of support that has meant so much to them is being cut off. It is a matter of great concern to them that therapists are now forbidden to help them. Even a man or woman who desperately wants to hold their marriage together is now denied the opportunity to seek to reduce their same-sex attractions.

The writing was publicly put on the wall in a letter to *The Independent* in 2010 by Professor Andrew Samuels, then Chair of UKCP:

---

3 http://www.rcpsych.ac.uk/rollofhonour/specialinterestgroups/gaylesbian/submissiontothecofe
psychiatryandlgbpeople.aspx <09 August, 2012>

4 UKCP's Guidance on the Practice of Psychological Therapies that Pathologise and/or seek to
Eliminate or Reduce Same-sex Attraction

'No responsible psychotherapist will attempt to "convert" a client from homosexuality to heterosexuality. It is clinically and ethically misguided. Any member of the United Kingdom Council for Psychotherapy who tried to do so would have to face the music.'[5]

Therapists are now 'facing the music'. And their clients, who have struggled long and hard against sexual feelings that they do not wish to have, will go to the wall – not because of science but for the sake of political correctness. The collateral damage for spouses and children will be immense.

A minority within a minority group, they cry for justice. On what grounds should they be denied the right to decide for themselves?

Dermot O'Callaghan

---

5 http://www.psychotherapy.org.uk/article1319.html

POSTSCRIPT – Finding Help

Are there aspects of any of these stories with which you can identify? Are you looking for greater freedom in issues relating to your own sexuality? You too may have experienced abuse, emotional or sexual, as a child or young person, or you might find yourself as an adult trapped in addictions of various types, including pornography.

You aren't alone.

Unfortunately finding the right help in the UK can be difficult because gay activists and those who support their agenda are determined to outlaw therapeutic help for those wanting to move quietly, honourably and respectfully out of homosexual practice.

You don't have to be a Christian to be in this position. You may have another faith or no faith. We all have the same human rights, to be able to live our lives as we see fit. No church, mosque, synagogue, counsellor or therapist has the right to push you in any direction you are not comfortable with. You may also choose to live in a gay relationship.

You have the right to decide.

One thing is certain, you can't do this all on your own, in isolation and feeling shamed because you are not where you want to be or feel you should be. Despite what you may be being told, there are individuals who can help you to work out what's right for you.

1. **Find a counsellor or psychotherapist** *who will work with your agenda*. Don't be afraid if they challenge you, but don't allow them to push to affirm homosexuality if this is not something you want to embrace.

2. **Find a caring church or community** with a *pastor or leader in whom you can confide, who does not shame you, and establish accountability* network for yourself. Make sure that it's a church or group which knows how to work with people who aren't perfect, and understand the principles of addiction and the value of community.

3. **If you can't find a professional** who supports your walk out of SSA, **don't be afraid to find another who is willing**

to work with you on *aspects of your personality that you know relate to your sexual issue*: perhaps exploring issues relating to self-esteem, assertiveness, family relationships, and relationship building. You don't have to tell them everything about yourself. You don't have to tell them what your goals are until they have earned your trust.

4. **Look for opportunities to join self-help groups or groups giving to others**. Groups where people are developing their skills, are involved in community projects, voluntary service opportunities, or hobbies are useful in your journey. We all need a sense of purpose and of being part of a community. Isolation is your enemy!

Mike Davidson